100 YEARS OF *Carefree Days* IN WEST MICHIGAN

Celebrating 100 Years of Tourism in West Michigan
1917-2017

100 Years of Carefree Days in West Michigan
ISBN: 978-0-692-80822-1
© 2017 West Michigan Tourist Association
Printed in Canada by Friesens

West Michigan Tourist Association (WMTA.org)

This book is made possible through the generosity of our sponsors: **Castle Farms** in Charlevoix (CastleFarms.com) and **Stafford's Hospitality**, with locations in Petoskey, Harbor Springs, Bay View, Alanson, and Charlevoix (Staffords.com).

Right: Winning photo of WMTA's 2016 West Michigan Photo Contest. Photo taken by Joel Bradshaw at Grand Haven Beach.

Welcome to West Michigan

West Michigan today is known throughout the country as a vacation paradise, blessed with a wealth of natural beauty, recreational opportunities, refreshing climate, and bountiful accommodations. But it wasn't always this way. At the turn of the 20th century, the lumber industry had plundered Michigan's forests and left vast cutover lands, with few agricultural prospects. The tourist industry was in its infancy. Visitors came by boat or train to specific places. Accommodations were provided in hotels, resorts, boarding houses or private homes, and cottages. Vacationers, usually on the higher end of the economic ladder, tended to stay in one locale, sometimes for the entire summer season.

While the steamship and railroad companies promoted travel to the areas they served, and some individual hotels and resorts advertised their services, there was not a central organization that promoted the tourist advantages of Michigan. The time was ripe in 1917 for the formation of the Michigan Tourist and Resort Association, now the West Michigan Tourist Association (WMTA), the first grass-roots tourist association in the country.

The arrival of the automobile and better roads brought many changes to the tourist industry. No longer were travelers tied to the timetables of the steamship or railroad companies. Automobiles

Van's Beach, Leland. Photo by Briana Paige.

gradually became more affordable, and vacation time more common. Travelers wanted information on places to visit, what to do, and where to stay.

The West Michigan Tourist Association stepped in to fill that need. Advertisements were placed in scores of newspapers across the Midwest. A wide range of publications were produced over the years, including tourist directories, maps, guides for golf, fishing, canoeing, winter sports, and more. Tours were arranged for travel writers, which resulted in free publicity in numerous newspapers.

With the launch of the WMTA website in 1997, much more information was made available, and is now updated continually.

Michigan's tourist industry is too often taken for granted. The growth of tourism in Michigan is indebted to the West Michigan Tourist Association for their efforts of promoting travel in our state for the last 100 years. With a legion of strong leaders, from Hugh Gray in 1917 to Dan Sippel in 2017, the WMTA has dedicated itself to the continued growth and enhancement of Michigan's vacation paradise.

Introduction by M. Christine Byron, Michigan Tourism Historian

Big Sable Point Lighthouse, Ludington. Photo by Selector Jonathon Photography.

1941 *Carefree Days in West Michigan* cover image.

West Michigan Through the Decades

1910s

1916

Arthur Stace from the *Grand Rapids Press* wrote a series of articles advocating for a central organization promoting tourism in Michigan.

1917

A meeting was called on May 7th at the Pantlind Hotel, with 75 delegates representing

Far Left: Fishing on the South Pier in St. Joseph in the early 1900s. Photo courtesy of The Heritage Museum & Cultural Center, St. Joseph.

Left: Albert Loeb, acting president of Sears Roebuck Co., purchased nearly 1,800 acres of property in Northern Michigan in June of 1917 and began construction on Loeb Farms (today known as Castle Farms), a model dairy farm modeled after the stone farms found in Normandy, France. Loeb Farms opened for business in 1918 as a working model dairy farm with over 200 dairy cows. In 1919, Loeb Farms opened its grounds for visitors, and became the largest employer in Charlevoix County, employing more than 90 people in its daily operations.

1910s

every county in West Michigan attending. The Michigan Tourist and Resort Association (MTRA) was formed as a non-profit corporation. Hugh J. Gray was hired as the secretary/manager. The organization was supported by memberships from resort owners, hotel proprietors, garage managers, retailers, newspapers, banks, and public utilities, as well as chambers of commerce and county boards of commissioners. Membership dues were $25 annually. This was the first grassroots tourist organization in the country.

1917-1918: U.S. engaged in fighting WWI.

Right: G.B. Russo opened his first East Grand Rapids store in 1905 with the goal of satisfying Italian immigrants' taste buds and introducing new products to Americans. Five generations of Russos have been dedicated to providing shoppers with the finest products and personal, knowledgeable service.

1910s

1918
The first MTRA money was spent on advertising in 33 newspapers in seven states.

MTRA's first booklet published: *Why Michigan? - Because*, written by Hugh Gray. Ten thousand copies were printed. Five thousand copies of an automobile map "inviting people to come to Western Michigan" were also printed.

With a state constitutional amendment, women won the right to vote in Michigan two years before the 19th Amendment to the U.S. Constitution granted the vote on a national level.

Michigan enacted prohibition of alcohol sales, two years before the national ban.

Left: Workers on the Robinette family farm in the early 1900s. The family bought the farm in 1911, opened the Apple Haus in 1973, and started their own winery in 2006, where they named their first hard cider after the farm's founder: Barzilla Robinette.

1910s

1919

The retail merchants of Grand Rapids gave space to the MTRA in the Morton House for an information bureau. A stereopticon machine ran in the evenings showcasing scenes of Michigan's attractions.

MTRA arranged that the state highway commissioner would furnish weekly bulletins regarding road conditions throughout Michigan to better answer questions from motorists regarding detours, etc.

MTRA suggested a tourist route loop of M-11 (now US-31) and M-13 (now US-131), which, if paved, would work together for a "dustless circuit." A naming contest for the route brought in 1,500 suggestions, including

Right: Map of the "Trunk Line Highways of Western Michigan," as published by the Western Michigan Development Bureau in 1918.

1910s

Peninsula Resort Circle, Rainbow Boomerang, Pumpkin Pike, Great Lakes Tour, Michigan Loop, Appleblossom Loop, Wolverine Drive, Scenic Reel, and Picturesque Tour.

Michigan State Parks Commission was established with D.H. Day as chairman. Hugh Gray anticipated the motor-camping craze of the 1920s and recommended that the state parks provide camping facilities, including such amenities as fresh water, firewood, and comfort stations.

The Upper Peninsula Development Bureau, which was founded in 1911, turned its focus away from agriculture and towards tourism.

The State Trunkline Highway System was created and highways were given numbers, whereas previously they were known by names.

Left: Photo of a man fishing in West Michigan, as featured in MTRA's 1919 guide.

1920s

1920
MTRA adopted a logo with a map of the lower peninsula, lettered in blue and yellow. Signs with the logo were made of enameled steel and hung in front of members' businesses.

1921
"The Playground of the Nation" was used extensively in advertising West Michigan. Grand Rapids advertised itself as the "Gateway to the Playground of the Nation." Traverse City called itself "The Heart of the Nation's Playground."

Far Left: Built in the 1920s by cereal baron W.K. Kellogg, the Kellogg Manor House on Gull Lake served as a summer home for the family, and today is open to the public for tours, luncheons, dinners, teas, weddings, and business meetings.

Left: The cover of the 1923 *West Michigan Vacation Directory.* The guide proclaimed that the Michigan Tourist and Resort Association had "nothing to sell except health and happiness."

1920s

MTRA opened a tourist information booth in Campau Square. It proved so successful that the City of Grand Rapids took over its operation the following year.

Encouraged by MTRA, the Michigan Department of Public Health inspected 109 summer resorts with a traveling laboratory to ensure safe milk supplies and sanitary conditions.

The "Ask Mr. Foster" travel agency in 16 southern cities distributed advertising materials from MTRA in the winter months.

1924
MTRA published the first *West Michigan Vacation Directory*. A page devoted

Right: Photo collage from the 1920 publication titled *Michigan: Along "The Great Lakes Way."* The publication boasted that "Michigan's pure, waterwashed air and invigorating climate give sound sleep, healthful rest, and absolute relief from hay-fever."

CREE LODGE ON DOUGLAS LAKE

CHILDREN IN THE SURF, TRAVERSE CITY

PICNIC GROUNDS, MICHILLI-MACKINAC PARK, MACKINAW CITY

HARBOR SPRINGS

SHORE DRIVE, NEAR CHARLEVOIX

INTERIOR VIEW, DANCING PAVILION, SAUGATUCK

WEST MICHIGAN

Vacation Directory

1920s

to information on the tour around Lake Michigan by way of the Mackinac Straits was the first promotion of what later became the *Lake Michigan Circle Tour*.

1926
The first meeting of the regional tourist organizations.

Henry Ford announced an eight hour, five day work week.

1927
MTRA conducted the first tour for Midwest travel writers. The tour highlighted attractions in West Michigan, and much publicity resulted from the four day tour. Other states soon copied the idea.

MTRA's survey showed that vacationers in Michigan bought supplies from local

Left: The 1926 cover of the *West Michigan Vacation Directory*, which was prefaced by a message from the Michigan State Medical Society urging travelers to "Add years to your life by coming to Michigan for your vacation."

1920s

businesses, including fishing tackle, bathing suits, and cameras, besides the essential gasoline and food.

MTRA initiated an autumn advertising campaign.

Charles Lindbergh, "Lucky Lindy," made the first non-stop flight across the Atlantic Ocean.

1928
Newaygo County was the first to promote fall color tours.

1929
MTRA's first out-of-state tourist information office was opened in Chicago.

MTRA sponsored a half-hour broadcast on Chicago stations WGN and WMAQ, and Cleveland station WTAM. The broadcasts opened with Irving Berlin's song, "I Want to Go Back to Michigan."

Right: The 1929 cover of the *West Michigan Vacation Directory*, touting West Michigan as "The Playground of a Nation."

West Michigan
"The Playground of a Nation"
Vacation Directory
1929

1920s

Hugh Gray of MTRA worked to develop funding for promoting tourism. The Rushton-Hartman Act created a State-funded and coordinated tourism development effort, which secured the first state appropriations for tourist advertising, amounting to $100,000 for advertising per year for two years, to be divided equally among the four regional tourist associations, and matched by each of them.

MTRA sponsored a postcard survey on tourism, which revealed that the average length of stay for vacationers was 18 days, and an average size of the parties was four persons. 42% stayed in hotels; 38% stayed at cottages; 14% camped.

MTRA sponsored a license plate contest, with hundreds of persons sending in lists of license plates from all 48 states. Winners were given cash prizes up to $40.

West Michigan
Vacation Directory

CAREFREE DAYS
in
WEST MICHIGAN

1930s

1930
The "Historic and Legendary Tour" of spots in West Michigan started in Grand Rapids and went as far north as Mackinaw City.

The Detroit-Windsor Tunnel opened to automobile traffic.

1931
MTRA created and distributed decals to be placed on automobiles bearing the inscription, "Guests of Western Michigan."

1932
MTRA published *The Visitors Guide of West Michigan,*

Far Left: The 1935 cover of the *West Michigan Vacation Directory*, which promised travelers "No matter how much or how little you have in your vacation budget, you can have a good time on that amount in West Michigan."

Left: The 1936 cover of *Carefree Days in West Michigan*, which included "The Log of a Motor Vagabond" to help encourage travelers to plan their own driving routes through the area.

1930s

a companion piece to the vacation directory.

1933

Hugh Gray's persistent efforts helped lead the National Forest Reservation Commission to approve the creation of the Manistee National Forest, which was formally dedicated in 1938.

Michigan's first Civilian Conservation Corps (CCC) was established in Chippewa County. The program continued through 1942.

Michigan was the first state to ratify the 21st Amendment, which repealed the prohibition of alcohol sales.

1934

The State Legislature created the Michigan Tourist and Resort Commission. To avoid

Right Top: The Lowell Centennial Celebration in 1931 at Recreation Park in Lowell.

Right Bottom: The second Lowell Showboat, as it looked in 1936.

Hotel Roselawn

1930s

confusion, the Michigan Tourist and Resort Association changed its name to the West Michigan Tourist and Resort Association (WMTRA).

1935
WMTRA informational offices were opened in Detroit, Cincinnati, Cleveland, and St. Louis.

The nation's first welcome center, established by the State Highway Department, opened in New Buffalo, near the Indiana border.

Left: Built in 1886, Stafford's Bay View Inn changed its name from The Roselawn in 1935. Stafford Smith first visited the inn in 1957 and returned each summer through 1960 to work a variety of positions. In summer of 1960, Stafford met and fell in love with his wife, Janice, who was working as a host in the dining room. Knowing the Bay View Inn had been recently put up for sale, Stafford and Janice became its new innkeepers. Stafford's Bay View Inn remains today the oldest summer hotel north of Grand Rapids.

1930s

1936

WMTRA moved into a new building located on Sheldon Ave. in Fulton Park.

WMTRA's annual publication, *Carefree Days in West Michigan*, replaced the *West Michigan Vacation Directory*. The Carefree theme, with few exceptions, continues in use today.

WMTRA, realizing that if Michigan were to continue to be a mecca for hay fever sufferers, something needed to be done to eradicate ragweed. They sponsored a ragweed eradication contest with a $5 bounty per county to the boy or girl destroying the largest amount of the weed. Some of the contestants

Right: A stone cairn monument was dedicated to Hugh J. Gray, the "Dean of Michigan's Tourist Activity," in 1938. Built of 83 stones, contributed by each of Michigan's 83 counties, it stands near the 45th Parallel on old US-31 near Kewadin in Antrim County.

CAREFREE DAYS
in
West Michigan

1939

1930s

destroyed as much as two and a half tons.

WMTRA amassed a library of 3,000 photographs, 20 reels of black and white film, and 10 reels of colored film. A three-week lecture tour through Florida the following winter was organized, showing the films to groups at major hotels, enticing them to visit Michigan.

St. Julian Winery, West Michigan's first winery, relocated from Windsor, Canada, to Paw Paw.

1938
By 1938, Michigan outranked even California in the tourist industry.

Left: The 1939 cover of *Carefree Days in West Michigan*, which encouraged visitors to use their camera on their trips, and suggested that "rail and stump fences, herds of grazing cattle, fields of grain, flocks of sheep, and broad beaches populated by happy bathers all make good color shots."

1940s

play and keep fit

1940

"Know Michigan Week" was organized by WMTRA to acquaint people with the growing importance of the tourist business to Michigan's economy. The campaign ran successfully for two years, but stopped as WWII progressed.

1941

From 1941-1945 the U.S. engaged in WWII. Auto plants and other factories were converted to the production of war materials, helping Michigan become known as the "Arsenal of Democracy."

Far Left: 1943's travel guide opens with the sentiment that "Certainly patriotic America is not thinking of having fun for fun's sake this summer," but reminds readers that vacations which "rest, relax, refresh, and revitalize" are essential to keeping fit.

Left: The 1942 edition of *Carefree Days in West Michigan*, encouraging wartime travelers "Sure, we've a lot of work to do, but we've got to keep fit to do it!"

"TRAVEL STRENGTHENS AMERICA"

1940s

1942

WMTRA's advertising during WWII promoted the idea that workers needed vacations to "keep fit to win," and that they should "spend a needed vacation in sunny-cool West Michigan."

Buses and railroads were available to take vacationers to resorts, where they were encouraged to "stay there rather than just travel." Travelers had to get along on tires made pre-war. It was one's patriotic duty to take care of their car as there were no new automobiles to buy. The last automobile manufactured for U.S. civilian use rolled off the assembly line in February.

Right: In 1942 as many as 60 barrage balloons were positioned closely together in the skies of Sault Ste. Marie in an effort to deter a bomb drop on the locks, and provide cover for the essential shipping system. Top photo courtesy Deidre Stevens, bottom courtesy U.S. Army Corps of Engineers.

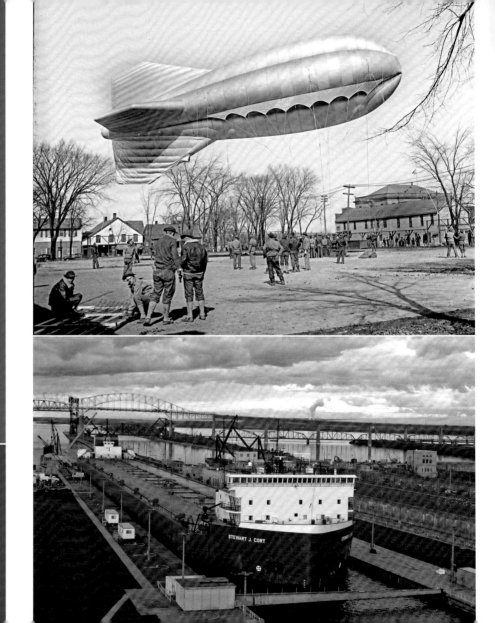

Carefree Days

IN

West

MICHIGAN

1940s

To counteract the effects of gasoline rationing, WMTRA proposed that steamers which had been making weekly pleasure cruises on Lake Michigan and Lake Huron be converted to common carriers to take tourists to various lakeshore resorts.

An emergency conference was called by WMTRA to appeal to the state to delay gasoline rationing in the Great Lakes region until at least Labor Day. This alternative to the suggested July 1st rationing would "protect the livelihood of people engaged in the $400,000,000-a-year industry."

1943
Hugh Gray died. William Palmer took over as secretary/manager of WMTRA through 1947.

Left: The 1944 cover of *Carefree Days in West Michigan*, which proclaims "We will win this war. The days of carefree, peacetime travel will come again."

1940s

1944
The Chicago office moved to 222 North Michigan Avenue, in the heart of "Travel Row."

WMTRA published an oversized map, *Tourist and Resort Map of West Michigan*, which listed resorts, hotels, etc.

1945
The Michigan Tourist Council was created, which included the secretaries of the four regional tourist associations, and it adopted an official logo, including the slogan "Tourist Empire of the Inland Seas."

1946
Greyhound Bus Lines expanded service to northern

Right: The 1945 edition of *Carefree Days in West Michigan* reminded wartime travelers to cooperate with their vacation hosts, who are "beset by many shortages," to have an enjoyable vacation. "If you have one little thing that doesn't please YOU, he has ten that HE would like to change."

Carefree Days

IN *West* MICHIGAN

CAREFREE DAYS
in
West Michigan

1940s

Michigan with two new routes.

West Michigan experienced a post-war vacation boom.

1948
Chester C. Wells took over WMTRA until his death in 1956.

The tourist industry ranked second only to the automotive industry in the state economy.

WMTRA proposed juggling Memorial Day and Labor Day dates to provide two three-day holiday weekends. (Congress did not act on this until 1968).

1949
A weekly news bulletin from WMTRA was made available to newspapers and radio stations describing snow, ice, and fishing conditions, weather forecasts, and a roundup of housing facilities available.

Left: The 1946 *Carefree Days in West Michigan* assured visitors that their "worries and tensions will fade away" on their visit to West Michigan.

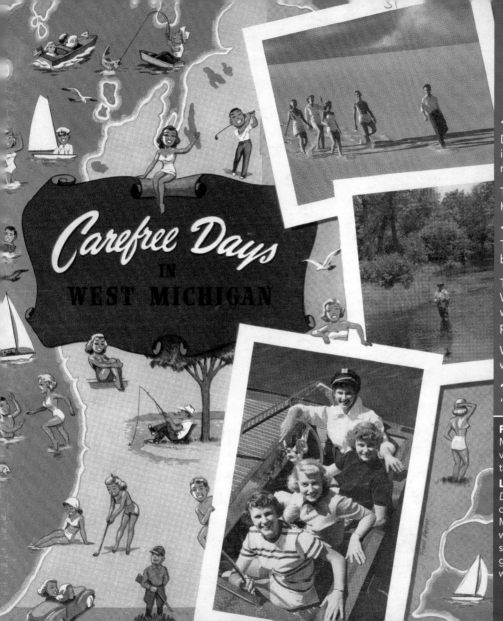

1950s

1950
Detroit was the 4th largest city in the United States, with 1.8 million residents.

The U.S. was embroiled in the Korean War from 1950-1953.

1953
Thirty-seven new motels were built in West Michigan.

The First Annual Governor's Winter Sports Conference was held, with WMTRA participating.

WMTRA published the first winter sports guide.

1954
"Michigan Week" was

Far Left: Shirley Swanson, Miss Michigan 1956, from Muskegon, visits Mac Wood's Dune Rides at the Silver Lake Sand Dunes.

Left: 1951 cover of *Carefree Days in West Michigan*, which details the natural beauty of West Michigan as "Sparkling lakes, white sand beaches, rippling trout streams winding through forest grandeur, and the majestic blue waters of Lake Michigan."

1950s

revived and continued as an annual tradition until it was abandoned under Jennifer Granholm's administration.

WMTRA, in cooperation with safety and highway agencies, sponsored a 31-county "Crusade for Safety" campaign, with 250,000 stickers given out to drivers to promote safe driving on Michigan's roads.

WMTRA called for state support of a historical sites program, noting the value of historical sites and markers as a tourist attraction. It also called for revival of the historical names of Michigan's highways and proper marking for memorial roads and historic trails.

WMTRA took credit, in part, for placing the slogan "Water Wonderland" on Michigan license plates.

Right: The annual Street Scrubbing at the Tulip Time Festival in Holland during the 1950s.

1950s

The first McDonald's was opened in Des Plaines, Illinois.

1955
WMTRA was awarded first place for Best U.S. Story and Photo Coverage of any area in the United States by the Midwest Travel Writers Association. In the two previous years, WMTRA placed second in the competition.

A bill sponsored by WMTRA which provided funds for the State Historical Commission to properly mark historic sites was passed by the state legislature.

1956
Leonard Gasoline became the principal sponsor of the television show *Michigan Outdoors* with Mort Neff as host. Free maps and brochures, *Going Places in Michigan*, were distributed

Left: Aurey Strohpaul of WMTRA accepted the Midwest Travel Writers' Award for Best U.S. Story and Photo Coverage. Photo courtesy Archives of Michigan.

1950s

through their service stations.

1957
Aurey D. Strohpaul assumed leadership of WMTRA until 1969.

WMTRA asked the state highway department for different colored signs to identify business routes off the new interstate highway system so that bypassed towns would not suffer unnecessary loss of business.

Mackinac Bridge opened for traffic on November 1st.

1958
Michigan ranked fourth in the nation in the tourist business, but tenth in the amount of

Right: The 1958 cover of *Carefree Days in West Michigan* celebrated the opening of the Mackinac Bridge. At 8,614 feet long, it was "by far the world's longest" when it opened, as well as the costliest, with a total price tag of $99,800,000. The bridge, in addition to linking the upper and lower peninsulas, became a tourist attraction in its own right.

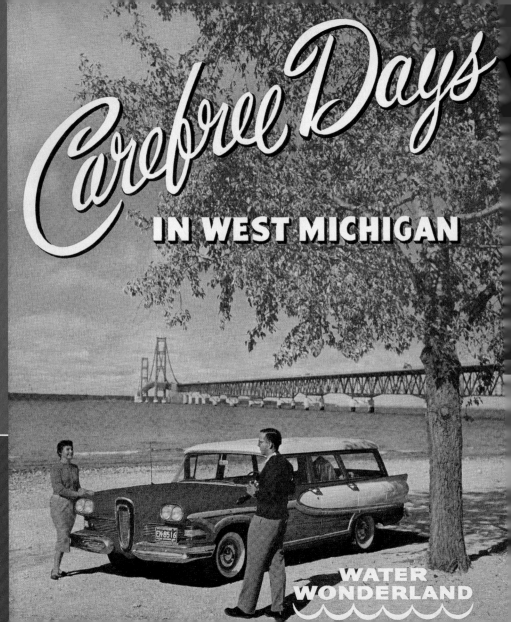

Carefree Days

IN WEST MICHIGAN

WATER WONDERLAND

1950s

promotional money spent to attract vacation revenue.

At a Michigan Public Service Commission hearing, Aurey Strohpaul of WMTRA testified on the importance of the rail service to the tourist industry. The Chesapeake and Ohio Railroad petitioned the commission to discontinue two daily passenger service runs between Grand Rapids and Petoskey.

1959
The St. Lawrence Seaway, linking the Atlantic Ocean to the Great Lakes, opened to shipping.

Motown Records was launched by Berry Gordy.

Left: Built in 1905 and substantially rebuilt in 1940, the S.S. *Milwaukee Clipper* is the oldest United States Passenger Steamship on the Great Lakes. Now housed permanently in Muskegon as a historic site, she is shown here on a voyage from Muskegon to Milwaukee in the early 1950s.

1960s

1960
The census revealed a 1.45 million population increase in Michigan, the largest in its history.

1961
West Michigan Tourist and Resort Association became West Michigan Tourist Association (WMTA).

WMTA pushed for a bill which would prohibit the sale of beverages in non-returnable containers.

1962
The U.S. Weather Bureau carried the WMTA ski reports on its teletype circuit.

The Cuban Missile Crisis raised the specter of a global nuclear catastrophe.

Far Left: Tourists flock to the Sleeping Bear Sand Dunes, circa 1962. Photo courtesy Phil Valyeat.

Left: The 1966 cover of *Carefree Days in West Michigan* highlights West Michigan's beaches, calling them the "vacation area's highlight attraction."

1960s

1963
The new State Constitution of Michigan was ratified.

1964
The Civil Rights Act of 1964 outlawed discrimination based on race, color, religion, or national origin in hotels, motels, restaurants, theaters, and all other public accommodations engaged in interstate commerce.

WMTA and Ontario participated in a joint advertising campaign for tourists bound for the 1964 New York World's Fair to take "The Great Lakes Route to the World's Fair."

The U.S. was deeply involved in the war between North and South Vietnam from 1964 to 1973.

1965
"Water Winter Wonderland"

Right: Children play in the sand on the shore of Lake Michigan, circa 1965. Photo courtesy Archives of Michigan.

1960s

replaced "Water Wonderland" on Michigan license plates.

1967
Michigan ranked as the number one attraction in the mid-U.S., and was among the "Big Four" for tourism, joining New York, Florida, and California.

WMTA's new slogan was "West Michigan is the Best Michigan."

The Michigan Senate praised WMTA, declaring that members of the legislature "extend their official recognition of the fiftieth anniversary of the association."

Alewives washing up on the shores of Lake Michigan caused an estimated $50 million of lost revenue from cancelled reservations. WMTA urged congress to declare

Left: The Whitehall/Montague Train Station in 1968, which has housed the White Lake Area Chamber of Commerce and Visitors Bureau since the early '80s.

1960s

the West Michigan beaches a "disaster area."

Coho fishing boomed on Lake Michigan. On a summer weekend, the Coast Guard estimated there were 6,200 boats on the lake between Manistee and Frankfort.

1968
Wesley B. Tebeau took leadership of WMTA through 1987.

Congress passed the "Uniform Monday Holiday Act" which moved four holidays from their traditional dates to a specified Monday in order to create three-day weekends.

Right: Willard (Bud) Ott (vice president of the WMTA board), William T. McGraw (State Tourist Council Director), and Governor William Milliken at the Chalet-on-the-Lake Resort near Stevensville. They filled bags with "Michigan Gold," Lake Michigan sand to be mailed by WMTA to the other 49 governors and travel writers in the Midwest. Photo courtesy Archives of Michigan, May 29, 1969.

1960s

WMTA made a suggestion to the National Weather Bureau that instead of predicting a 20% chance of showers, the bureau should predict an 80% chance of sunshine.

1969
WMTA moved into new offices at 136 E. Fulton. The building was remodeled for the "Hospitality House" in a colonial decor specific for WMTA.

WMTA took Governor William Milliken coho fishing on Lake Michigan, where he vowed to eat a coho (even if he did not catch one himself), to "calm down those sports fishermen who might be concerned by the DDT scare."

Left: Walt Disney visits with Donald Gilmore at the Gilmore Car Museum in Hickory Corners and learns to drive a vintage Model T. Visitors to the museum today can step inside the giant movie set from *The Gnome-Mobile*, one of the only Disney movie sets to leave their studios.

WEST
MICHIGAN

1970s

1970

WMTA sponsored a survey to study the economics of snowmobiling. It was estimated that there were at least 75,000 snowmobiles in the state.

Wes Tebeau of WMTA joined Governor Milliken on an inspection tour of pollution problems in Benton Harbor, Muskegon, and Grand Rapids. Tebeau commented that "So far we have not been able to develop a campaign that will induce vacationers to swim in a sewer, camp in a dump, or enjoy a beach littered with broken bottles."

Sleeping Bear Dunes National Lakeshore was established,

Far Left: The 1972 West Michigan *Carefree Days* encouraged visitors to "cut loose for the best West Michigan vacation ever."

Left: Waterskiiers from the 1970 edition of *Carefree Days in West Michigan*, photographed at Pennellwood Resort in Berrien Springs.

1970s

although it was not formally dedicated until 1977.

1972
"West Michigan's Super Spring" campaign was launched by WMTA to promote off-season business.

WMTA published *West Michigan Historic Lighthouses*.

1973
WMTA urged winter vacationers to vacation close to home or use buses due to the gasoline shortage.

1974
WMTA promoted winter surfing in conjunction with the Great Lakes Surfing Association.

Right: 50,000 stickers were distributed by WMTA in 1971 with the annual *Carefree Days* in a campaign promoting "super hospitality." The circular stickers feature a psychedelic design and proclaim "Michigan Loves Me - West Michigan Tourist Association Told Me So." Photos courtesy of Grand Rapids Public Library.

1970s

Two new Michigan Tourism out-of-state information centers were established in Chicago and Cleveland.

PA-263 was passed, allowing counties to levy a tax to fund tourism promotion and development activities.

Gerald R. Ford of Michigan became the 38th President of the U.S.

1975
The State Highway Department announced plans for 68 rest areas along the state's expressways. An experimental program was inaugurated, permitting directional signage of resorts and other tourism-related business within a prescribed distance from the site.

Left: Children with dog on toboggan from the *Carefree Days* 1973 skiing edition. Photo courtesy Archives of Michigan.

1970s

An airline strike had a positive effect on Michigan tourism as vacationers chose to travel by auto to closer locations.

The ore freighter, *S.S. Edmund Fitzgerald*, sank in Lake Superior during a storm with all aboard lost.

1976
WMTA, in cooperation with the other three regional tourist associations, distributed 240,000 specially "minted" "Tourist Buck Bills" to its members as part of a campaign to make the Michigan business community aware of the $3.91 billion impact of tourism. Members were urged to mail a tourist dollar with every check they wrote for goods, services, food, beverages, and

Right: The *Carefree Days* winter edition from 1976 included information for travelers interested in "skiing, snowmobiling, tobogganing, or yodeling from a mountain top."

WEST MICHIGAN
TOURIST ASSOCIATION

CAREFREE DAYS

SKIING
Tobogganing
X-COUNTRY
Snowmobiling

WEST MICHIGAN
carefree days

**Spring-Summer-Fall
Vacation Attractions**

MARCH 1979

1970s

payroll to show the power of the tourism industry. An enterprising reporter put a bogus bill in a machine and got a dollar in change. WMTA sent a notice to its members to trim the bills so they wouldn't "fit in money machines and hit jackpots."

To celebrate the U.S. Bicentennial, WMTA published a Bicentennial historic touring map of West Michigan, listing 111 points of historic interest.

Throwaway bottles were banned by a referendum vote in Michigan.

1977
Michigan again ranked second only to California in tourist outdoor travel, and sixth nationally in all types of travel.

Left: The 1979 edition of *Carefree Days* urged visitors to "Please remember to treat our land with kindness and respect. Keep it beautiful for all the children to come."

MARCH 1980

SPRING SUMMER
FALL VACATION
★ ATTRACTIONS ★

1980s

1980

Governor William G. Milliken declared 1980 as "Michigan Year of the Coast" in recognition of the major importance of the Great Lakes to the state's commerce and industry, tourism, recreation, and water supplies.

A Congressional Tourism Caucus was established in the House of Representatives with 111 members. The purpose of the caucus was to "develop more awareness of the importance of tourism to the economy and to promote tourism."

WMTA sponsored a "Tourism Study Trip" to Ixtapa, Mexico, for members.

Far Left: The 1980 cover of *Carefree Days in West Michigan* shows off the view from Fort Mackinac on Mackinac Island.

Left: The Michigan Flywheelers Museum in South Haven opened in 1983, dedicated to the restoration and preservation of antique gas and steam engines and tractors.

1980s

1981
WMTA sponsored a "Tourism Study Trip" to the Cayman Islands for members.

Michigan ranked 7th in populations among the 50 states.

1982
The "Say Yes to Michigan" campaign was launched in January during the big game.

1984
Carefree Days included an eight-page full color photo spread featuring "West Michigan's Palette," showcasing the area as a "festival of mood and color."

Detroit Tigers won the World Series.

WMTA's *Outdoor Guide* included a "first-timer's guide to the fun and thrill of Lake

Right: The 1981 *Outdoor Guide* featured information on fishing, canoeing, camping, hunting, parks, forests, and fall color.

CAREFREE DAYS IN WEST MICHIGAN

1981 OUTDOOR GUIDE

CANOEING
CAMPING
FISHING

CONTENTS PAGE 4

1980s

Michigan sport fishing."

1985
The *Carefree Days* vacation guide included information on "American Plan" resorts, which offered all-inclusive stays for vacationers.

More nautical traffic passed through the Soo than through the Panama and Suez Canals combined.

The *West Michigan Outdoor Guide* included a "Camping Cuisine" article, offering "a mouth-watering look at some tasty alternatives to campers' hot dogs & beans."

1986
Carefree Days included an article focusing on tips for better picture taking by John Penrod, a top Michigan photographer.

Left: Located on a bluff 70 feet above Lake Michigan in South Haven, Lake Bluff Inn and Suites opened in 1980, promoting their "breathtaking sunsets."

1980s

"Fan mail" from guests who enjoyed their stays at West Michigan B&Bs was reprinted in *Carefree Days*, including comments of "Would like to keep you a guarded secret!!" and "Your rooms were old-fashioned and charming...like Grandma's house."

1987
Michigan celebrated 150 years of statehood.

Carefree Days included information on Michigan's Recreational Harbors.

1988
Gary C. Fisher assumed leadership of WMTA through 1994.

The first *Lake Michigan Circle Tour* guide was published, and continued as the *Lake Michigan Circle Tour and Lighthouse Guide.*

WMTA published the *West Michigan Canoeing Map & Guide* and *West Michigan Golf Map & Guide.*

1980s

Carefree Days included recipes from West Michigan Bed and Breakfasts.

The *Carefree Days Camping Guide* included an article titled "Is Full-Time RVing for You?" targeting retirees.

1989
The Berlin Wall, which had separated the city of Berlin for 27 years, fell.

WMTA published three new maps: Attractions/Festivals, Boating/Fishing, and Camping.

Left: The Coopersville & Marne Railway Company was incorporated on July 13, 1989. The track through Marne and Coopersville was first laid down in the summer of 1858. The first train into Grand Rapids arrived in June of 1858, with the first train into Grand Haven arriving in September of that year. The Coopersville & Marne Railway Company now provides passenger excursions, with themed rides centered around various holidays.

WEST MICHIGAN
WM
TOURIST ASSOCIATION

1990s

1990

WMTA set a new record with 475,000 pieces of travel literature printed and distributed.

WMTA no longer received state funds to operate, and became a self-sustaining, membership-based association while maintaining a non-profit status.

WMTA published *West Michigan Fall Fun & Color Tour Guide*.

1990-1991: War in the Persian Gulf region.

1991

The Union of Soviet Socialist Republics (USSR) dissolved.

Far Left: Hobie Cats line up on South Haven beach for a sailing regatta, as featured on the 1990 travel guide cover.

Left: New Holland Brewing opened in Holland in 1997, and has since grown to offer a wide variety of beer, whiskey, gin, rum, vodka, and liqueur at brewpubs in Holland and Grand Rapids.

1990s

WMTA's annual guide was renamed *West Michigan Travel Planner*.

The *West Michigan Travel Planner* included an article on West Michigan Lighthouses, accompanied by a map of their locations.

1992
WMTA's annual guide was renamed *West Michigan Travel Guide*.

Information on winery tours and tastings was provided to WMTA callers.

1993
A guide to the Hart-Montague Bicycle Trail was distributed through WMTA.

The *West Michigan Travel Guide* included over 500

Right: Built in 1993, Chateau Chantal gets much of its fruit from the Begin Orchards plants, which originally occupied the area. The building was expanded in 2003 to include a Bed and Breakfast attached to the winery.

1990s

listings on its Event Calendar, spanning from April through October.

The European Union was formed.

First World Wide Web browser developed at the University of Illinois.

1994
The Michigan Travel Bureau was renamed Travel Michigan, and was transferred from the Department of Commerce to the Department of the Michigan Jobs Commission. The Michigan Travel Commission was likewise transferred.

West Michigan Travel Planner included a "Fun Index"

Left: Grand Rapids' Amway Grand Plaza Hotel in the early 1990s. Originally built as the Pantlind hotel in 1913, the glass tower was added in 1983 and the building reopened as the Amway Grand Plaza Hotel. Visitors today can take a self-guided history tour of the hotel.

1990s

which listed everything from Antiques to Zoos.

1995
William (Bill) DeHaan assumed leadership of WMTA for two years.

1997
Linda Singer became Executive Director of WMTA until 2003.

The website WMTA.org was launched.

WMTA offered "Spring Break" kits which suggested activities at museums, zoos, and nature centers, and also included one-day and overnight getaways.

Travel Michigan created a new logo featuring a lighthouse, orange sun and blue waves and the slogan "Great Lakes. Great Times." Welcome signs with the new logo were placed

Right: The 1993 *West Michigan Travel Guide* included a "Fun Index" and a photo journey through West Michigan.

1993 EDITION

West Michigan
TRAVEL GUIDE

WEST MICHIGAN
wm
TOURIST ASSOCIATION
QUALITY · SERVICE · VALUE

1990s

at various points of entry into Michigan.

1999
WMTA published the *West Michigan Golf Guide*, which was continued intermittently with similar titles.

The *Fall Fun & Color Tour Guide* included driving instructions for 23 fall color routes, as well as a highlight of historic covered bridges in the area.

West Michigan Travel Guide included a section of "Elsewhere in Michigan & Nearby States."

Left: For more than 100 years, vacationers have made their way to a certain spot on the shore of northern Michigan's Little Traverse Bay in Petoskey. That spot was a natural paradise with a reputation as the perfect vantage point for viewing the "million dollar" sunsets over Lake Michigan. In 1998, that site became home to the Inn at Bay Harbor, designed in homage to the grand hotels of the late 19th century.

WEST MICHIGAN
Carefree Travel

2000s

2001

WMTA's annual guide was now called *West Michigan Carefree Travel*. An expanded "Quick-Finder" section included entertainment, corporate facilities, and many vacation rentals. Over the years, other special sections featured pet-friendly accommodations, farmers markets, and museums.

A "Farm Market Quick Finder" was included in the *West Michigan Carefree Travel Guide*, detailing farms' locations and offerings.

Terrorist attacks occurred at the World Trade Center in New York City and the Pentagon in Washington, D.C.

Far Left: Opened in 2009, Nancy Anne Sailing Charters offers sailing charters and sunset cruises on Lake Macatawa in Holland.

Left: The 2005 *West Michigan Carefree Travel Guide* included detailed driving routes for 26 fall color tours.

2000s

Travel nationwide slowed because of the sluggish economy, which was made worse by the September 11th terrorist attacks. Many travelers were inclined to stay closer to home. Seventy percent of travelers to West Michigan were state residents.

Gas prices topped $2 per gallon, reaching a "psychological barrier," and had a dampening effect on tourism.

WMTA added listings of haunted attractions to their website.

2002
Michigan's first female governor, Jennifer Granholm, was elected.

Right: The JW Marriott Hotel in Grand Rapids opened in 2007 adjacent to the historic Amway Grand Plaza hotel. The Amway building incorporates the original Pantlind Hotel from 1913, where the meeting to form the West Michigan Tourist Association was held in 1917.

2000s

The *West Michigan Carefree Travel Guide* included an article on "Wine Tasting 101" for the 600,000 visitors to wineries in the region each year.

Detroit Red Wings won the Stanley Cup.

2003
The United States led an invasion of Iraq and ousted Saddam Hussein.

Richard (Rick) Hert took over as WMTA's Executive Director until 2015.

2005
West Michigan Carefree Travel included a "Lake Michigan Circle Tour Lighthouse Directory."

2006
The "Pure Michigan" slogan was created by the McCann Erickson advertising agency for Travel Michigan and an advertising campaign was carried out regionally.

2000s

WMTA listed St. Patrick's Day events and lodging packages on their website.

2007
The "Pure Michigan" campaign received the Mercury Award for "Best State Tourism Advertising Campaign" and "Best State Television Commercials."

WMTA published a special 90th Anniversary Edition of *West Michigan Carefree Travel* with a history article and timeline of the past 90 years.

Right: The Outdoor Discovery Center Macatawa Greenway is a non-profit education and conservation organization that was founded in 2000. Their purpose is to connect people with nature through outdoor education for the benefit of wildlife and the conservation of the natural world. More than 75,000 people annually visit their sites to walk the trails and view the wildlife. The organization now protects over 1,200 acres along the Macatawa River in Ottawa County and a 150 acre preserve in Fillmore Township.

2000s

2008

Due to the recession, tourism index hit the lowest level in nine years at the end of 2008.

The *Lake Michigan Circle Tour & Lighthouse Map* was redesigned from a booklet into a fold-out poster-sized map.

2009

Michigan's tourism industry outperformed the rest of the state's economy, due in part to the Pure Michigan campaign, which was launched nationally this year. *Forbes* magazine placed "Pure Michigan" sixth-best among the top ten all-time travel campaigns.

Left: The Felt Estate opened to the public in 2007 after major renovations to restore the mansion and grounds. Originally built in 1928, the grounds and mansion served as a private residence, a seminary, and a state prison, before falling into a state of disrepair and being restored by volunteers from Laketown Township and surrounding communities.

FOUR SEASONS OF FUN

2010s

2010

Governor Granholm signed legislation transferring $10 million from the 21st Century Jobs Fund to pay for the successful Pure Michigan advertising campaign. The money was in addition to the $5.4 million allotted to the tourism campaign in the fiscal year 2011.

WMTA's annual guide featured a section on agritourism.

2011

Sleeping Bear Dunes National Lakeshore was voted "Most Beautiful Place in America" by ABC's *Good Morning America* television show viewers.

Far Left: ArtPrize 2012 "Lights in the Night" entry in Grand Rapids. Photo courtesy of Kevin Povenz.
Left: A special section in the 2012 *West Michigan Carefree Days* promotes fun in West Michigan in all four seasons.

2010s

The *Carefree Travel Guide* included information on local shops throughout West Michigan where travelers could find unique souvenirs.

2012
The *Carefree Travel Guide* promoted a new sport on Michigan's waterways: Stand Up Paddleboarding.

Girlfriend Getaways and Mancations were highlighted in the annual guide as unique vacation options.

2014
Farm to Table dining was highlighted in the annual *Carefree Travel Guide*, showcasing the growing trend in West Michigan.

Right: Winning photo of the inaugural 2014 West Michigan Photo Contest, which was featured as the cover image of the 2015 *Carefree Travel Guide*. Photo taken by Rachel Gaudette at Ludington State Park.

2010s

The inaugural West Michigan Photo Contest was launched by WMTA.

2015
Dan Sippel began his current tenure as Executive Director of WMTA.

Governor Snyder promoted Pure Michigan as a tourist destination during the China Investment Mission.

Michigan continued to grow its reputation as a state with great local foods, wine, and craft

Left: What once was the Belden Brick and Supply in Holland has been transformed into an authentic distillery and tasting room: Coppercraft Distillery, established in 2012. The distillery is part of the still-growing movement in West Michigan and creates premium small-batch spirits by hand using local ingredients. Coppercraft adds their spirits to classically inspired cocktails which genuinely complement the spirits with freshly pressed juices, locally grown herbs, and other house-made ingredients.

2010s

beers. CNN called Traverse City "one of seven up-and-coming foodie destinations," while Grand Rapids claimed the title "Best Beer Town" in *USA Today*.

2016
Dan Sippel took a group of

Right: Michigan's Heritage Park opened in Whitehall in 2015. Traveling through the heritage park takes visitors through 10,000 years of Michigan History in a natural woodland setting. Become a paleontologist and help unearth a mastodon at the dig site. Experience daily life in a Native American Wigwam Village (1650). Interact with a fur trader (1760) stocking his shelves in the Fur Trade Post. In the Settlers Cabin (1830), learn about the life of early settlers and help with daily chores. Visit with Civil War Soldiers (1861 to 1865) in their winter camp. Stretch out on a bunk in the Lumber Shanty (1880) and learn what "small game in the bunk" means. Find out what it took to put dinner on the table in the Farmhouse (1900) and learn what the Civilian Conservation Corps (1933) did in Michigan.

2010s

Chinese travel writers on an eight-day 1,000-mile tour through West Michigan.

Gold Coast Sunsets were highlighted in the annual *Carefree Travel Guide*, with advice on the best places in West Michigan to watch a sunset over Lake Michigan.

2017
WMTA celebrates 100 years of promoting tourism in West Michigan.

Left: Following a passion for Farm-to-Table dining in West Michigan, Grove restaurant opened in Grand Rapids in 2011. Grove considers the best dining a celebration of honest food and the local people who are passionate about growing, raising, preparing, and savoring the bounty of the earth's harvest. Grove believes the most flavorful food begins with the highest quality ingredients, which is why they responsibly source as much as is available from local, family, and sustainable farms and businesses.

Fishtown, Leland. Photo by Jeff Simonis.

West Michigan Today

Sleeping Bear Dunes, Leelanau. Photo by Selector Jonathon Photography.

Upper Peninsula waterfall. Photo by Jerry Hamberg.

Grand Haven Lighthouse. Photo by John Hill.

Grand Haven Channel. Photo by Jodi Leslie.

Morel Mushroom in Grand Haven. Photo by Laura Hilliard.

Castle Rock, Munising. Photo by Jerry Hamberg.

Six Lakes fishing tournament. Photo by Rory Bancroft.

Silver Lake area in Mears. Photo by Todd Maertz.

Silver Beach in St. Joseph. Photo by Laurie Schmidtke.

Deerlick Park Beach in South Haven. Photo by Sheryl Kaptur.

The Blockhouse in Muskegon State Park. Photo by Tim Bonnette

MUSKEGON STATE PA
DESIGNED AS A SCENIC
BUILDING WAS COMPLE
BY THE CIVILIAN CONS
DESTROYED BY FIRE I
BLOCKHOUSE WAS R

Ludington State Park Beach. Photo by Lisa Schaap.

Acknowledgments

Thank you to Chris Byron and Tom Wilson from Vintage Views Press for their countless hours of WMTA research, trips to the archives, and contributions to WMTA's history timeline.

Thank you to the State Archives of Michigan and Grand Rapids Public Library for assisting us with accessing their archives.

Thank you to the participants of past West Michigan Photo Contests, for allowing us to reproduce your photos in the "West Michigan Today" section of this book.

Thank you to our sponsors, Stafford's Hospitality and Castle Farms, for making this book possible. Please see more about our sponsors on the following pages.

More West Michigan

For more information on the West Michigan Tourist Association and West Michigan destinations, please visit our website at WMTA.org or connect with us on social media.

Left: Lake Michigan/Lake Macatawa channel at Holland State Park. Photo by Veronica Bareman.

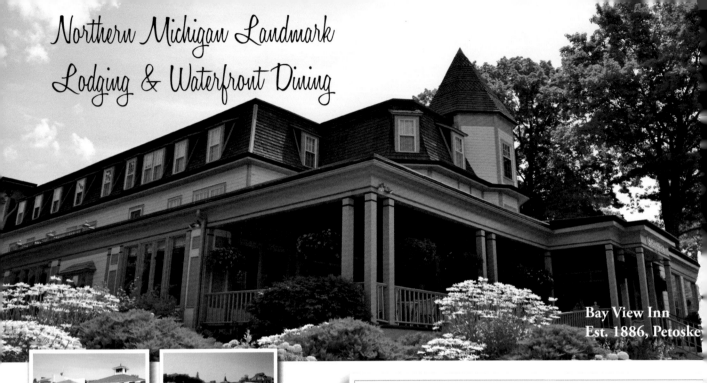

Northern Michigan Landmark Lodging & Waterfront Dining

Bay View Inn
Est. 1886, Petoske

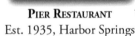

PIER RESTAURANT
Est. 1935, Harbor Springs

WEATHERVANE RESTAURANT
Est. 1871, Charlevoix

PERRY HOTEL
Est. 1899, Petoskey

CROOKED RIVER LODGE
Est. 2004, Alanson

Where Yesterday & Today Come Together

Stafford's has provided premier waterfront dining and historic lodging throughout northern Michigan, welcoming visitors to the crown jewel of Michigan's "Gold Coast" for over fifty-five years.

We invite you to join in the heritage of hospitality that we continue to practice every day for every guest in relaxed, historic settings. Learn more at staffords.com.

STAFFORD'S